THE
HUMAN BODY

The Facts Book for Future Doctors

Biology Books for Kids Revised Edition | Children's Biology Books

BABY PROFESSOR

Revised Edition, 2019

Published in the United States by Speedy Publishing LLC, 40 E Main Street, Newark, Delaware 19711 USA.

© 2019 Baby Professor Books, an imprint of Speedy Publishing LLC

Baby Professor Books are available at special discounts when purchased in bulk for industrial and sales-promotional use. For details contact our Special Sales Team at Speedy Publishing LLC, 40 E Main Street, Newark, Delaware 19711 USA. Telephone (888) 248-4521 Fax: (210) 519-4043. www.speedybookstore.com

10 9 8 7 6 * 5 4 3 2 1

Print Edition: 9781541968264
Digital Edition: 9781541968509
Hardcover Edition: 9781541968400

See the world in pictures. Build your knowledge in style.
https://www.speedypublishing.com/

Contents

THE HUMAN BODY'S
MAIN STRUCTURES
6

THE FIVE SENSES
10

ORGAN SYSTEMS
14

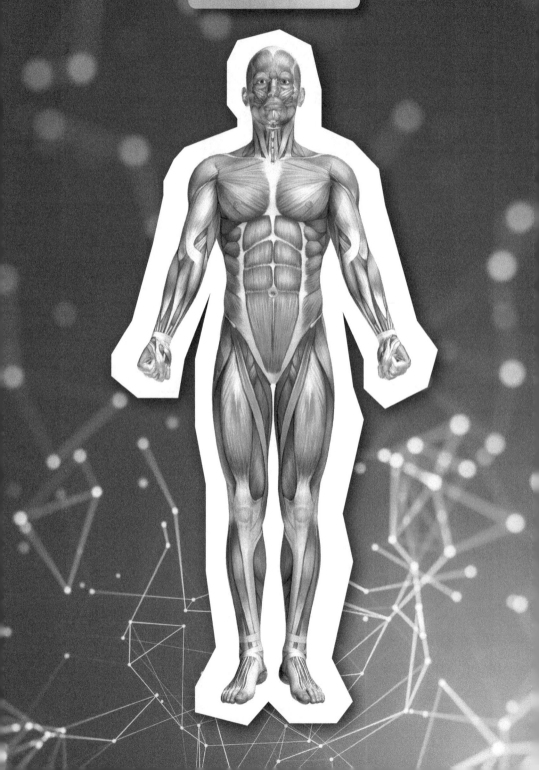

In this book, we're going to talk about the human body. So, let's get right to it!

The human body is a very complicated maze of systems. Each system has its own types of cells, different types of tissues, and various organs. Biologists generally organize the study of the human body into varying systems depending on their functions. If you want to be a doctor in the future, you would study all eleven organ systems. You have to know the human body inside and out in order to keep your patients healthy. Most doctors learn all these systems and then become specialists in a certain system of the body. For example, a cardiologist is a doctor who specializes in diseases of the heart and circulatory system.

THE HUMAN BODY'S MAIN STRUCTURES

If you look at a picture of the human anatomy, you see the main structures very quickly. The human head houses the brain, which controls all the body's systems. The head also contains the organs for seeing, for hearing, for smelling, and for tasting. You can experience touch with your head as well. For example, when you place your head down on a soft pillow, you're experiencing touch with your face. Most of the time we touch things with our hands, but the skin everywhere on your body can experience touch.

The other main structures besides the head are the neck and the torso, also called the trunk, and your arms and legs. Your neck and torso include many of the vital systems and most of the internal organs that keep you functioning every day. Your arms and legs help you to get from one place to another by walking, running, jumping, or swimming.

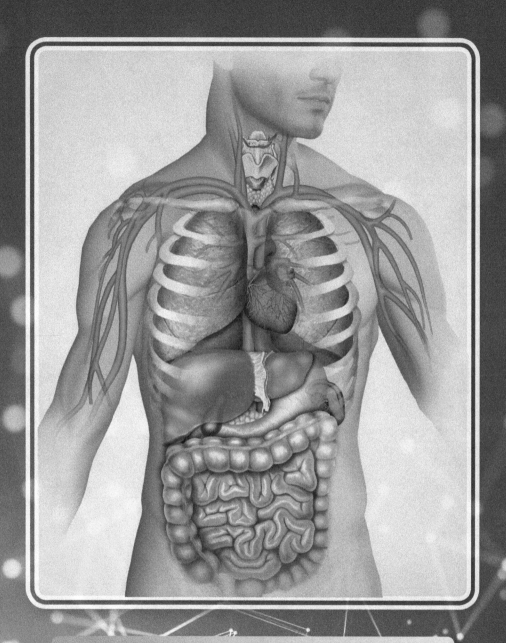

THE NECK AND TORSO INCLUDE MANY OF THE VITAL
SYSTEMS AND MOST OF THE INTERNAL ORGANS

Our bodies have five senses that help us to absorb information about the environment around us. These senses help to keep us safe and send information to our brains so that we can experience everything around us.

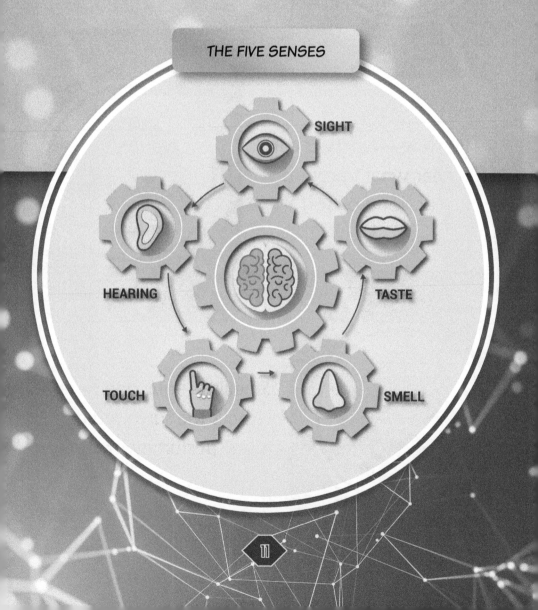

THE FIVE SENSES

SIGHT

HEARING

TASTE

TOUCH

SMELL

Sight—our two eyes
see what's around
us, close or far

Hearing—our two ears
hear what's around
us, loud or soft

Smelling—our one nose
smells the surrounding
odors, perfumey or stinky

· Taste ·

Tasting—our taste buds on our tongue detect, sweet or salty

Touching—our skin and especially our hands detect, smooth or rough

· Touch ·

ORGAN SYSTEMS

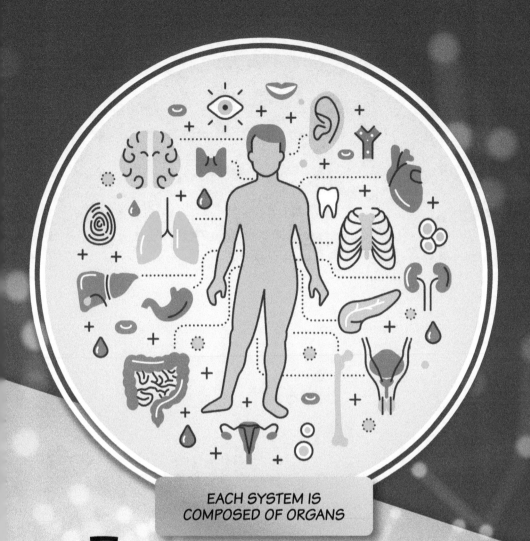

Each of the systems in the human body is composed of organs and other body structures. Each system has a special function to perform in keeping us alive and healthy.

Skeletal System

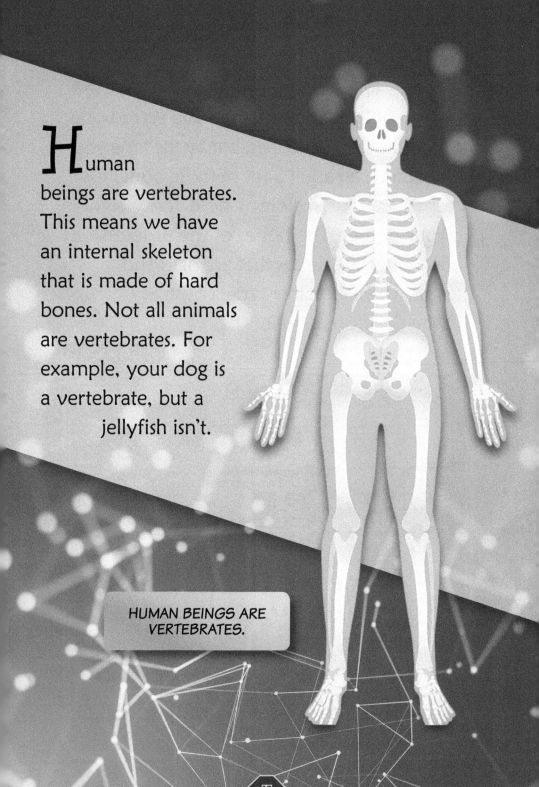

Human beings are vertebrates. This means we have an internal skeleton that is made of hard bones. Not all animals are vertebrates. For example, your dog is a vertebrate, but a jellyfish isn't.

HUMAN BEINGS ARE VERTEBRATES.

The human skeleton is composed of 206 bones. When you were born you had 270 bones, but by the time you become an adult a lot of those bones fuse together. Our skeletons hold the weight of our bodies. The bones of the skeleton are connective tissues that are rigid and tough. There are other types of tissues in the skeleton as well.

THE HUMAN SKELETON IS COMPOSED OF 206 BONES.

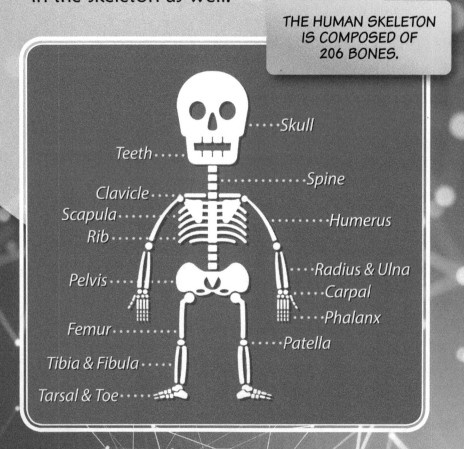

Skull
Teeth
Spine
Clavicle
Scapula
Rib
Humerus
Radius & Ulna
Carpal
Phalanx
Pelvis
Femur
Patella
Tibia & Fibula
Tarsal & Toe

We also have
cartilage. One
of the places we have
cartilage is in our noses.
The cartilage bends slightly so
you can tell it's not as hard as bone.
The other important components of our
skeletons are our joints. Joints connect bones
together. They can also connect bone with
cartilage. The third possibility is when
joints connect cartilage with
cartilage.

Muscular System

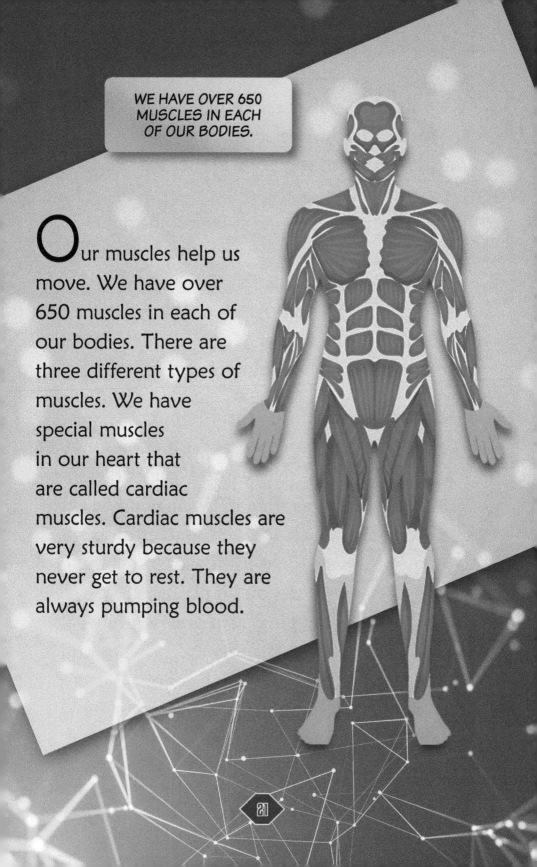

Our muscles help us move. We have over 650 muscles in each of our bodies. There are three different types of muscles. We have special muscles in our heart that are called cardiac muscles. Cardiac muscles are very sturdy because they never get to rest. They are always pumping blood.

We also have skeletal muscles that attach to our skeletons. These muscles expand and contract so we can move. Many of our muscles are built in pairs so that when one expands, the other one contracts. The third type of muscle is called smooth muscle. Smooth muscles are inside our organs. For example, smooth muscles line the walls of our stomachs and allow them to expand based on how much food we're eating.

Muscles sometimes move because we consciously tell them too, but sometimes they do things automatically without our conscious control. In other words, if you want to get up out of a chair, you'll send a conscious message to your muscles to tell them to help you stand up. If you're sleeping at night, your heart and other organs are still working even though you're not consciously commanding them.

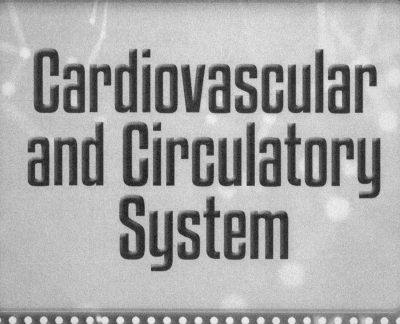

Cardiovascular and Circulatory System

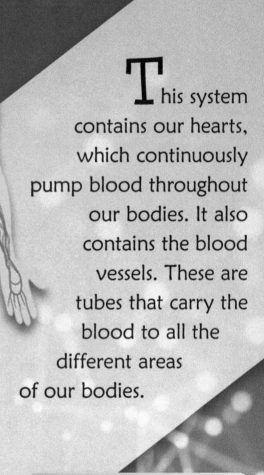

This system contains our hearts, which continuously pump blood throughout our bodies. It also contains the blood vessels. These are tubes that carry the blood to all the different areas of our bodies.

CARDIOVASCULAR AND CIRCULATORY SYSTEM CONTAINS OUR HEARTS AND BLOOD VESSELS.

THE ARTERIES ARE THE TUBES THAT CARRY THE BLOOD.

The blood that flows through our arteries and veins carries the life-giving oxygen as well as the nutrients our cells must have to survive. The arteries are the tubes that carry the blood that is pumped from the heart to all the body's systems. Arteries have to be strong as well as thick because the heart puts them under quite a bit of pressure as the blood flows. When a nurse feels your pulse, she has her fingers on one of your arteries. Veins carry the blood that's already been used for oxygen and nutrients back to the heart.

Digestive System

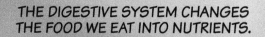

THE DIGESTIVE SYSTEM CHANGES
THE FOOD WE EAT INTO NUTRIENTS.

The function of our digestive system is to change the food we eat into the nutrients our body can process so that we have the energy to live, move, work, and play. Some of the major organs of our digestive system are:

The stomach, which breaks down our food using special enzymes

The small intestine, which continues to break our food down into nutrients

The large intestine, which pushes the waste materials through our systems so we can eliminate

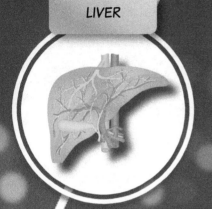

The liver, which provides bile that transforms fat into smaller pieces

The pancreas, which helps us digest by providing specialized enzymes

Nervous System

The nervous system is composed of the brain, the bundled nerves that are enclosed by your spine, which is called the spinal cord, and the huge network of interconnected nerves that cover the entire body. The brain, along with the spinal cord, make up the central nervous system. The remaining nerves are the peripheral nerves.

THE BRAIN AND THE SPINAL CORD MAKE UP THE CENTRAL NERVOUS SYSTEM.

You can think of the nervous system as a type of communication system for the body. Our brains control our muscles through motor nerves. Signals from our five senses travel through the sensory nerves so the brain can interpret what we're experiencing.

Respiratory System

The function of the respiratory system is to inhale oxygen into the body and once it's used, exhale the waste product of carbon dioxide. Human beings need oxygen to live. The main organs in this system are the lungs. They are essentially sacs that fill with fresh air and absorb it like a sponge absorbs water. Blood is pumped into the lungs' walls by the heart. The blood takes in the oxygen and then emits the carbon dioxide. When you breathe out, the waste product of carbon dioxide is released from your body.

Endocrine System

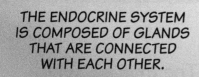

This system is composed of glands that are connected with each other. They emit special hormones that control and help regulate a lot of the functions of your body. This system includes:

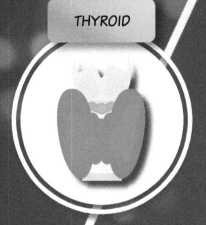

The thyroid, which controls our metabolisms, this is essentially how quickly we use the energy from our food

The pancreas, which is part of both the digestive and endocrine systems, controls the level of sugar in the blood

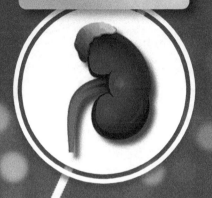

The adrenal glands, which control blood pressure

The pituitary gland, which affects human growth

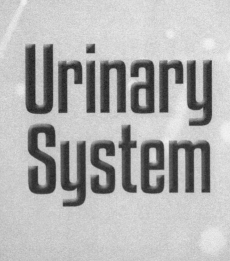

Urinary
System

The urinary system is composed of the kidneys as well as the bladder. You have two kidneys. They are each about the size of a fist and are bean-shaped. The kidneys' job is to filter the blood for impurities, which go out of your body through two tubes. These tubes transport the urine to your bladder. Inside the bladder the urine collects until you are holding about 2 cups. Then a signal is sent to your brain that tells you it's time to find a bathroom so you can empty your bladder through the urethra.

Immune and Lymphatic System

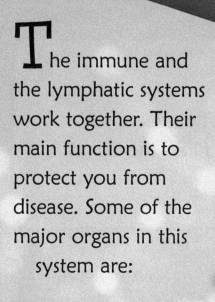

The immune and the lymphatic systems work together. Their main function is to protect you from disease. Some of the major organs in this system are:

THE IMMUNE AND LYMPHATIC SYSTEMS PROTECT YOU FROM DISEASE.

SPLEEN

The spleen, which filters the blood

LYMPH NODES

The lymph nodes, which help to fight infection

The thymus, which protects the body from germs and other toxins

BONE MARROW

Bone marrow, which produces blood cells

Reproductive System

The reproductive system consists of the organs that make it possible for babies to be born. These organs are different in males and females.

THE REPRODUCTIVE SYSTEM MAKES IT POSSIBLE FOR BABIES TO BE BORN.

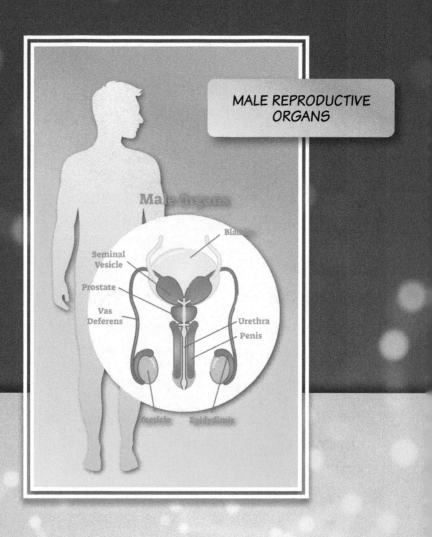

Male Organs

Bladder

Seminal
Vesicle

Prostate

Vas
Deferens

Urethra

Penis

Testicle   Epididymis

In men, the urethra is part of the urinary system as well as the reproductive system. It carries urine, but it also carries sperm in semen. The testes produce the sperm.

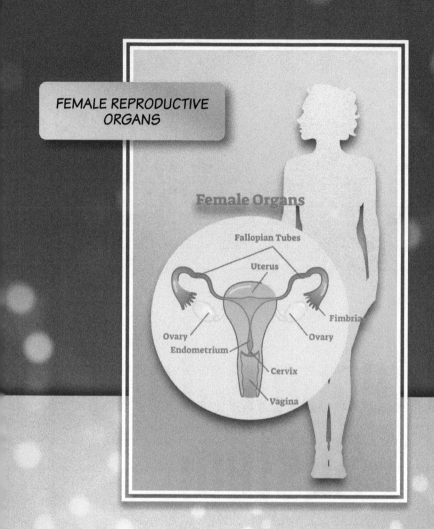

Female Organs

Fallopian Tubes

Uterus

Fimbria

Ovary

Ovary

Endometrium

Cervix

Vagina

In women, the vagina is connected to the uterus. The uterus is connected to two ovaries. When a woman gets pregnant, the uterus holds the developing baby, which is formed when a man's sperm and a woman's ova unite.

Integumentary System

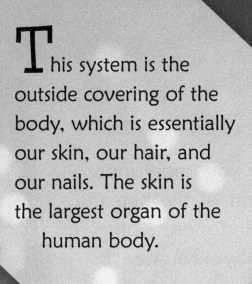

This system is the outside covering of the body, which is essentially our skin, our hair, and our nails. The skin is the largest organ of the human body.

THE INTEGUMENTARY SYSTEM IS THE OUTSIDE COVERING OF THE BODY.

Awesome! Now you know more about the systems of the human body. You can find more Biology books from Baby Professor by searching the website of your favorite book retailer.

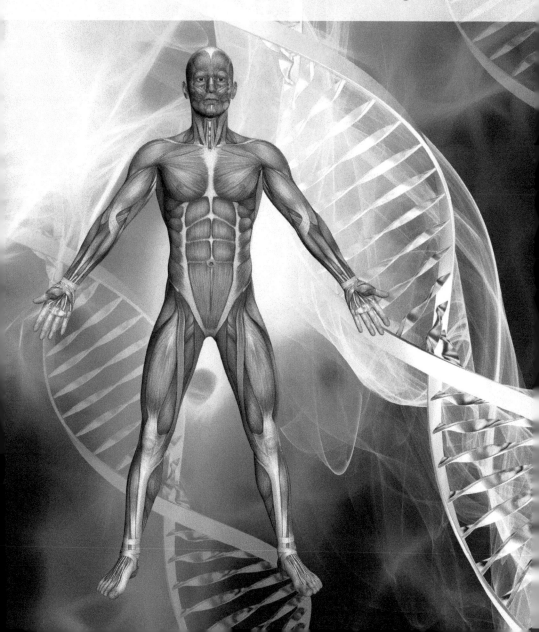